Women
and the
Priesthood

Alice von Hildebrand
and
Peter Kreeft

FRANCISCAN UNIVERSITY PRESS
Franciscan University of Steubenville
Steubenville, Ohio

"The Mystery of Femininity: Why It Excludes the Priesthood"
© 1994 by Alice von Hildebrand. All rights reserved

"Why Only Boys Can Be the Daddies: A Summary of the Arguments against Priestesses"
© 1993 by Peter Kreeft. All rights reserved

Printed in the United States of America

1994 Publication by:
Franciscan University Press
Franciscan University of Steubenville
Steubenville, Ohio 43952

Cover Design*: Dawn C. Harris

*The symbols on the cover are universal symbols for female and male.

ISBN 0–940535–72–6

Contents

I

Why Only Boys Can Be the Daddies

A Summary of the Arguments against Priestesses

by Peter Kreeft

Introduction

The last time I taught a course on C. S. Lewis to two hundred students at Boston College, nearly all of the students agreed with nearly everything he wrote in a dozen books and a dozen articles that we read—except one thing. Most of the students not only disagreed with, but felt very strongly that Lewis was outrageously out of line in opposing priestesses in his very wonderful article "Priestesses in the Church?"

The issue looms large—too large, I think, at least compared with the apocalyptic, cosmic, spiritual war we are in. As Pope John Paul II has said, "The eclipse of God has descended massively on the Western world." And yet there is a connection between this larger issue and the smaller one. Next to abortion, women's ordination is the most polarizing and passionate issue in the Church today. I do not think that I or an angel from heaven could convince and convert the one-third who are passionately committed to the cause for priestesses. But a sorting out and summarizing of reasons against priestesses and for the Church's teaching may help sway the one-third who are not passionately committed to either side, and it would be helpful for the one-third who are committed to the Church's position to take an inventory of their intellectual weapons. That is my purpose here. I do not think I have any new arguments, just restatements of others' arguments. Here is my attempt at a succinct summary of the Church's case for the controversial proposition "Only boys can be the daddies!" (That, straight from "Mr. Rogers' Neighborhood.")

I shall present only one side of the issue—the Church's side—because the arguments on the other side are very simple and very obvious. They come down to "Why not?" The idea of priestesses is not "guilty until proven innocent" but "innocent until proven guilty." The onus of proof, it seems, is on the Church's side. I will accept that onus of proof and try to prove the idea guilty.

Before looking at the substantive arguments, however, I think it is useful and honest to look at ourselves and our prejudices because they are, in fact, operative in the discussion. Four, in particular, move us today, all in the direction of saying yes to women's ordination: the power of positive thinking, egalitarianism, guilt about male chauvinism, and the desire for peace.

Our Prejudices

First, we always prefer positive thoughts and feelings to negative ones; we would rather say yes than say no. But God gave us "no" as well as "yes." Ann Landers defines "personality" as the ability to say yes, and "character" as the ability to say no. We need both. We need negativity, limits, narrowness, borders—or else nothing will have definition and character. Without the negative, no positive.

We especially hate limitations that make us suffer—poverty, disease, weakness. I think God must have arranged our lives to be full of lived limits like these partly because without such limits, there is no drama. One of the saddest things about being filthy rich, I imagine, is the lack of limits. The rich can do nearly anything and, therefore, their lives lack drama and bite. They always have a much higher suicide rate than the poor. The one society on earth with a zero suicide rate is the poorest and most primitive society on earth—the Australian aborigines. So it behooves us to say a preliminary hurrah for limits and barriers, and a yes to "no," in principle. But in fact we say the opposite.

Second, we—especially we Americans—are egalitarians. We hate discrimination. But discrimination is one aspect of limit, of "the no." God discriminated between men and women in creating us different. We may rebel against this, but it is rebelling against our own nature. Already, by nature and the will of the Creator, men are barred from getting pregnant and birthing children. And women are barred from impregnating. God is just, but God's justice is far greater and richer and more mysterious than mere equality. God's justice is harmony, like music—not mathematics, like an equation. The ancients understood this justice because they lived in a natural cosmos, not a man-made and artificial one surrounded by technological and political complexities and artifices.

Human justice has a rightful concern for equality because we need to protect ourselves and our rights against others who, like the fascists, would impose an unnatural and unjust inequality on us. But we also need to protect ourselves against those who, like the communists, would impose an unnatural and unjust equality on us. It is simply not true that deep down we are all the same. The deeper down you go, the more the you find the secret of uniqueness. Ultimately, we find the difference between the heavenly and the hellish, the thoroughly and successfully human and the thoroughly and eternally inhuman, deep down.

In the Book of Genesis, not all discrimination and differentiation is between good and evil. God introduces distinctions into creation, including the distinction between male and female, for good. In fact, each act of creation is an act of discrimination: light from darkness, waters below the firmament from waters above the firmament, land from sea, living from non-living, animal from plant, birds from fish, one species from another, man generically from animals, and male from female.

The third prejudice is that we men today are especially sensitive to women's demands out of guilt, a double guilt. First, guilt for past scorn and prejudice against women as inferiors by many of our fathers. Second, guilt for present, dehumanizing violence, raping, and battering by our brothers. But our fathers and our brothers are not us. We are not personally responsible and guilty for their sins against women. Yet though we may not rightly feel guilt for these sins, we do naturally and rightly feel shame, for they are our fathers and brothers. It is "all in the family." If you found that Adolf Hitler was literally your grandfather, you would naturally feel shame for this black sheep in your family. Now we want to relieve this shame and compensate for these wrongs, as affirmative action tries to compensate for slavery, or as a professor bends over backwards to give a good grade to a student he dislikes and has been unfair to. The danger here is over-compensation, responding to past injustice by present opposite injustice, trying to make a right by two wrongs.

A fourth and less praiseworthy motive than the well-meaning but misdirected attempts to compensate for past wrongs is the fear of present trouble; the lust for comfort; giving in to intimidation; the fanatical desire not to be seen as a "fanatic"—or modernity's other f-word, "fundamentalist." "Get those pushy, pesky feminists off our backs; give them what they want!" Americans, especially American administrators, including many Church administrators, usually have a tremendous desire to be accepted, to be accommodating, to be nice. As Bill Cosby says about parents, "We don't want justice, we want quiet!"

But these considerations decide nothing; they just warn us. What decides the issue is good arguments. Rather, what should decide the issue—any issue—is good arguments. I assume, perhaps naively, that my readers still believe in the existence and desirability of objective truth, and the power of human reason to know it and even, sometimes, to prove it. If that faith is dead, so is civilization. Barbarism defeats all civilization very effectively, just as a bull defeats a china shop. I think this is the bottom line of Nietzsche's "Will to Power" philosophy and of its progeny today, deconstructionism.

The Arguments

There are at least four kinds of reasons, four essential arguments, against priestesses: reasons of authority; reasons of sexual symbolism; reasons of the ecclesiastical common good; and reasons of discernment. The first set is composed of arguments which are the simplest of all: the authority of God, the authority of Christ, and the authority of the Church.

Reasons of Authority

God is the one who invented the priesthood, and who calls to the priesthood. The Church did not invent the priesthood. She received it. In fact, the Catholic Church claims less authority than any other Christian church in the world. That is why she is so conservative, so "stuck in the mud." Protestant churches feel free to change the "deposit of faith" (e.g., by denying Mary's assumption), or to change the "deposit of morals" (e.g., by allowing divorce, though Christ clearly forbade it—cf. Mk 10.1–12; Lk 16.18), or to change the essence of the liturgy (e.g., by denying the Real Presence and the centrality of the Eucharist in worship which was constant throughout the Church's first fifteen hundred years. That historical discovery, by the way, played an enormous role in my own conversion from Protestantism). The Church will not change the priesthood because she cannot. She is not its author, or even its editor, only its mail carrier.

The Catholic priesthood was not the first priesthood that God invented. He created two others before it—the Levitical priesthood, which was superseded and set aside by Christ, and the priesthood of Melchizedek, which was fulfilled by Christ. Just as the Jews were not free to institute priestesses, neither are Catholics. None of these priesthoods can be chosen or demanded or changed by man (or woman). Christ said, "You have not chosen me, I have chosen you" (Jn 15.16).

The chosen people of the Old Covenant did not establish the Jewish priesthood. It was established by the Supreme Being who limited the priesthood to males of the tribe of Levi. Did God then unjustly discriminate against members of the other eleven tribes, both men and women? Shall we accuse God of sin? What an absurdity! God picks his priests, and they serve at his pleasure. When Korah and other non-Levites tried to perform priestly rites, Moses warned them. When they continued in their obstinacy, God destroyed them (cf. Nm 16).

Christ on earth established the Catholic priesthood, the priesthood of the New Covenant. Man had no more say in this than in the Levitical priesthood. Christ purchased the right to set the laws and limits for his sacraments, including Holy Orders, with his own blood on the Cross.

Christ chose only males to be apostles. Why?

Advocates of priestesses say that he bowed to cultural limitations, to deep-seated, ancient male chauvinism. I wonder how many understand the arrogance of this idea. Imagine the absurdity of accusing Jesus Christ of the sin of sexism! Or, if he was not a sexist himself, but tolerated sexism in deliberately choosing only male apostles, then he compromised with and fostered this sin. To believe such arguments is to deny the Incarnation, the essence of the Christian faith.

The feminist view of Jesus does not fit the pattern we find throughout his life. He was never afraid to offend smaller and greater sensibilities than this one—for instance, when his disciples ate with unwashed hands, and when he told the Jews that they must drink his blood. So why would he succumb only to this one prejudice?

In addition to the authority of God in the Old Testament and of Christ in the New, there are nearly two thousand years of uniform Church teaching and practice of priestesslessness. Even on a purely human and secular level, that is an impressive vote by what Chesterton calls "the democracy of the dead."

The same Chesterton, always brimming with common sense, warns us that if we don't understand the reason for some ancient tradition or institution, that is good reason for not abolishing it. If you were to come across a strange building in an unexpected place, it would be really foolish to knock it down because you didn't understand its purpose. You may take it down only if you do understand its purpose and that it is no longer needed. Advocates of priestesses freely admit that they don't understand why the "males only" rule applies to the priesthood. Well, we do. So using Chesterton's common sense criterion, the only people who might have a right to change the old rule are exactly the people who don't want to change it, and the people who don't have a right to change it, because they don't understand it, are exactly the people who do want to change it.

The Church calls herself our *mater et magistra,* mother and teacher. Let's have no *mater si, magistra no* from Right or Left. The Church is not judged by human ideologies, but vice versa. To be a Catholic is to believe that the Church is more than a human institution, that she is graced with Christ's real presence and promise of guidance into all truth. I have never met a single advocate of priestesses who faced and affirmed that fact and manifested the loyal and loving submission all the saints had to our mother and teacher. When feminists become saints, we will become their pupils.

My position is no a priori prejudice against change in the Church. She is a living body, and therefore grows. But she grows from within, like a vine, not from without, like a machine or an ideological platform. And as I shall show in my second main point, the change to priestesses would manifest not organic growth and maturity but an identity crisis.

It is a simple and massive fact that the Church has said no to priestesses—consistently, publicly, clearly, and authoritatively. "Rome has spoken; the case is closed"—that formula used to evoke love and loyalty, not snide sneers.

The issue today is not whether the Church will have priestesses. She won't. The only open issue is whether the would-be priestesses will have the Church. The issue is not theoretical but practical; it is a test of loyalty to the Church, and therefore to Christ. For the Head is not related to his Body as a CEO to a business, but as the furry ball between your shoulders to your torso. To say yes to Christ but no to his Church is to will a divine decapitation.

Today's rebels against the Church's authority on this issue (or others) nearly always misunderstand the very essence of authority. They think it means power, but it means right. In fact, it means "author's rights." Christ, the Author of the Church, has rightful authority over his own Body, his own organs—unless we are not his Body, not sheep but goats. His sheep follow him—follow him, not lead him—because they know his voice, recognize his authority.

This is all we need say about the issue. The case is closed. We can be certain of what is true and right here, even if we do not understand the Church's reasons. But the Church, like a good mother, also gives us reasons. She tells us not only "Do this because Mommy says so," but also "Mommy wants you to know why she says so."

Reasons of Sexual Symbolism

Her main reasons comprise my second point.

The first two things we learn about sex from God, right from the beginning, are that God designed it, not man or society, and that it is very good. The first command was, "Be fruitful and multiply." I do not think God had in mind growing oranges and memorizing times tables. It is significant that most advocates of priestesses do not seem to believe or care much about this. Feminists usually see sexuality as a social, human, conventional, changeable thing, and radical feminists usually see it as a problem, an obstacle, or even an enemy, when they rail against the "prison" of having wombs. The next step is natural: glorifying the act of breaking out of this "prison" by killing their unborn babies. If they see their bodies and their sexuality as theirs and not God's, it is quite natural that they should proceed to the next step of seeing their babies as theirs and not God's.

Advocates of women's ordination usually misunderstand sexual symbolism because they misunderstand symbolism itself as radically as they misunderstand authority. They think of symbols as man-made and artificial. They do not see that there are profound and unchangeable natural symbols, that *things* can be *signs.* Saint Thomas Aquinas based his multiple method of scriptural exegesis on this eminently sound but tragically forgotten principle. He writes: "The author of Holy Writ is God, in whose power it is to signify His meaning, not by words only (as man also can do) but also by things themselves. So whereas in every other science things are signified by words, this science [sacred science] has the property that the things signified by the words [of Scripture] have themselves a signification. Therefore that first signification, whereby words signify things, belongs to the first sense, the historical or literal. That signification whereby things signified by words have themselves a signification is called the spiritual sense, which is based on the literal and presupposes it."[1]

In other words, God writes history (and nature) as man writes words. Behind St. Thomas's hermeneutic is a metaphysics—the sacramental view of nature and history. Thomas Howard has brilliantly pinpointed the difference between the ancient world-view, in which everything means something, and the reductionistic modern worldview, in which nothing means anything, in *Chance or the Dance?* If every thing in nature means something, then the big things in nature mean something big. And sex is a Big Thing. What it means is so big that we will never exhaust it, only discover more facets of its diamond. But it is there, a massive fact of nature, not a clever human idea.

Every good poet knows that natural symbols are like the essential structures of language itself, unchangeable. The sky is, always was, and always will be a natural symbol for heaven; dirt is not. The eye's seeing is a natural symbol for the mind's understanding; the gut's groaning is not. We all know and recognize this unconsciously. That is why our language has evolved as it has. We use "see" to mean both literal, physical seeing and symbolic seeing or understanding. Ascending, light notes in a major key somehow *have* to mean hope and joy; descending, heavy notes in a minor key inevitably mean something grave. Words like "grave" and "gravity" have multiple meanings glued with inextricable mental epoxy. Everything is connected, and everything points beyond itself—especially sex. God, who deliberately designed sexuality, also deliberately designed to incarnate himself as a male. Jesus Christ is still a male. He still has his human body in heaven. It is and forever will be a male body. This is not ideology or theology or interpretation; this is fact, this is data. What follows is my attempt to explain the Church's "no" to priestesses in light of this data.

My explanation can be summarized in two propositions. First, priests of Christ who are Christ's mouths through which he himself says, "This is my Body," must be men because Christ is a man. Second, Christ, the perfect human image of the Father, is male because God is Father. To deny my first proposition is to deny the Eucharist, and thus Catholicism. To deny my second proposition is to deny the authority of Christ, and thus Christianity.

C. S. Lewis—not a Catholic himself—saw point one better than most Catholics do:

Why should a woman not in this [priestly] sense represent God? . . .

Suppose the reformer stops saying that a good woman may be like God and begins saying that God is like a good woman. Suppose he says that we might just as well pray to 'Our Mother which art in Heaven' as to 'Our Father'. Suppose he suggests that the Incarnation might just as well have taken a female as a male form, and the Second Person of the Trinity be as well called the Daughter as the Son. Suppose, finally, that the mystical marriage were reversed, that the Church were the Bridegroom and Christ the Bride. All this, as it seems to me, is involved in the claim that a woman can represent God as a priest does. . . .

. . . Christians think that God Himself has taught us how to speak of Him. To say that it does not matter is to say . . . that all the masculine imagery is not inspired, is merely human in origin. . . . And this is surely intolerable: or, if tolerable, it is an argument not in favour of Christian priestesses but against Christianity. . . . It is also surely based on a shallow view of imagery. . . .

. . . One of the ends for which sex was created was to symbolize to us the hidden things of God. One of the functions of human marriage is to express the nature of the union between Christ and the Church.[2]

The priesthood does not mean merely ministry. The new ICEL mistranslations of the liturgy which substitute "minister" for "priest" are blind to the blindingly obvious fact that a priest is not just a minister. Ministries like lector, eucharistic minister, teacher, psychologist, counselor, social worker, and political activist—and even prophet—are indifferent to sex. Women can and do perform them. But priesthood is different. Only a priest can consecrate. A Catholic priest is not just a symbol of Christ (even that would form a strong argument against priestesses) but is sacramentally *in persona Christi.* When he says, "This is my body," we hear Jesus Christ speaking. Father Murphy does not mean "This is Father Murphy's body"! The priest is not merely remembering and repeating Christ's words here; he is really "channeling" them. The ICEL-proposed revisions of the Roman Missal, rejected by the bishops in November 1993, substituted "presbyter" (elder) and "presider" for "priest"; and eliminated references to God as "Father."

Christ's priests are men because Christ is a man.

But why is Christ's maleness essential? Because he is the revelation of the Father, and the Father's masculinity is essential. This is the second half of our equation.

To understand this second proposition, we must distinguish "male" from "masculine." Male and female are biological genders. Masculine and feminine, or yang and yin, are universal, cosmic principles, extending to all reality, including spirit.

All pre-modern civilizations knew this. English is almost the only language that does not have masculine and feminine nouns. So it is easy for us who speak English to believe that the ancients merely projected their own biological gender out onto nature in calling heaven masculine and earth feminine, day masculine and night feminine, sun masculine and moon feminine, land masculine and sea feminine. In the Hindu marriage ceremony the bridegroom says to the bride, "I am heaven, you are earth." The bride replies, "I am earth, you are heaven." Not only is cosmic sexuality universal, its patterns are suspiciously consistent. Most cultures saw the sun, day, land, light, and sky as male; moon, night, sea, darkness, and earth as female. Is it not incredibly provincial and culturally arrogant for us to assume, without a shred of proof, that this universal and fairly consistent human instinct is mere projection, myth, fantasy, and illusion rather than insight into a cosmic principle that is really there?

Once we look, we find abundant analogical evidence for it from the bottom of the cosmic hierarchy to the top, from the electromagnetic attraction between electrons and protons to the circumincession of divine Persons in the Trinity. Male and female are only the biological version of cosmic masculine and feminine. God is masculine to everything, from angels to prime matter. That is the ultimate reason why priests, who represent God to us, must be male.

There is striking historical evidence for this in the Jews, God's chosen people, the people to whom God revealed himself (and if we do not believe that, we do not believe in *that God,* for that is the only place we find *that God*). The

Jews, and the Christians and the Muslims and the philosophical theists who learned from them, were radically different from all the others in their concept of God in five related ways.

First, they worshipped no goddesses, and no bisexual or neuter gods. The Jews' only God was always He, never She or It.

Second, they had no priestesses.

Third, the Jewish God was utterly transcendent to the universe, for he created it out of nothing. There is even a word in Hebrew that is not in any other ancient language: *bara'*, "to create." Only God can do it, not man. This God was not a part of the universe, as in polytheism, or the whole or the soul of the universe, as in pantheism.

Fourth, God spoke. He revealed himself in prophetic words and miraculous deeds. He came out of hiding and acted. All other religions were man's search for God. Judaism (and Christianity, its fulfillment) was God's search for man. Therefore, religious experience for a Jew was fundamentally response, not initiative. There were no yoga methods, no ways to push God's buttons. God initiated, man responded.

Fifth, the Law was the primary link with God, who revealed his will in Thou Shalts and

Thou Shalt Nots. The god of pantheism may have a consciousness, but not a will; and the gods of polytheism have conflicting and sometimes evil wills. Only in Judaism is there a full union of religion and morality. Only the Jews united mankind's two primary spiritual instincts—the instinct to worship and the instinct of conscience. Only the Jews identified the object and end of worship with the Author of conscience and morality.

These five remarkably distinct features of ancient Judaism are clearly connected. As a man comes into a woman's body from without to impregnate her, God creates the universe from without and performs miracles in it from without. He also calls to man, reveals himself and his law to man from without. He is not The Force but The Face; not Earthspirit rising but Heavenly Father descending; not the ideal construct of man's mind but the Hound of Heaven. To speak of "religion" as "man's search for God," if we speak of this God, is like speaking of the mouse's search for the cat (to steal an image from C. S. Lewis).

This issue is absolutely central, and therefore I beg your indulgence while I quote a long paragraph from Lewis, which I believe is the best single paragraph ever written on the difference between Christianity and man-made religions:

> Men are reluctant to pass over from the notion of an abstract . . . deity to the living God. I do not wonder. Here lies the deepest tap-root of Pantheism and of the objection to traditional imagery. . . . The Pantheist's God does nothing, demands nothing. He is there if you wish for Him, like a book on a shelf. He will not pursue you. There is no danger that at any time heaven and earth should flee away at His glance. If He were the truth, then we could really say that all the Christian images of kingship were a historical accident of which our religion ought to be cleansed. It is with a shock that we discover them to be indispensable. You have had a shock like that before, in connection with smaller matters—when the fishing line pulls at your hand, when something breathes beside you in the darkness. So here; the shock comes at the precise moment when the thrill of *life* is communicated to us along the clue we have been following. It is always shock-

ing to meet life where we thought we were alone. 'Look out!' we cry, 'it's alive'! And therefore this is the very point at which so many draw back—I would have done so myself if I could—and proceed no further with Christianity. An 'impersonal God'—well and good. A subjective God of beauty, truth and goodness, inside our own heads—better still. A formless life-force surging through us, a vast power which we can tap—best of all. But God Himself, alive, pulling at the other end of the cord, perhaps approaching at an infinite speed, the hunter, king, husband—that is quite another matter. There comes a moment when the children who have been playing at burglars hush suddenly: was that a real footstep in the hall? There comes a moment when people who have been dabbling in religion ('Man's search for God'!) suddenly draw back. Supposing we really found Him? We never meant it to come to that! Worse still, supposing He had found us?[3]

The fundamental problem with most advocates of priestesses is as radical as this: they do not know who God is. Most would register strong discomfort or puzzlement at the description Lewis gives of God—i.e., the Bible's God.

Now, if the reply is that this ancient biblical picture of the hunter-king-husband God is historically relative, and that we should throw away the accidental shell and keep the essential, timeless meat of the nut, I reply:

First, the masculinity of God is not part of the shell, but part of the nut. It is not like Hebrew grammar, a translatable and replaceable medium. Something as deliberate and distinctive and as all-pervasive in Scripture as God's he-ness is no mere accident, especially when so obviously connected with the other four points of the five-point complex noted above.

Second, if it is a residue of the sin of sexism, then God has revealed himself sinfully. This really denies the existence of divine revelation. Or it judges the divine revelation by human ideology and opinion rather than vice versa, thus frustrating the very purpose, the essential purpose, of revelation, which is to reveal something that we could not have come up with from our own opinions or ideologies, to correct them.

Behind the idea of the need for divine revelation is the idea of Original Sin—another traditional notion which most priestess-advocates deny, ignore, or at least are very embarrassed at. We are not good and wise and trustable, but sinful and foolish and in need of correction, so we should *expect* to be surprised and even offended by God's revelation; otherwise, we wouldn't need it.

Third, there is the "camel's nose under the tent" argument. Once you start monkeying with your data, where do you stop? Why stop, ever, at all? If you can subtract the divine masculinity from Scripture when it offends you, why can't you subtract the divine compassion when that offends you? If you read your Marxism into Scripture today, why not your fascism tomorrow? If you can change God's masculinity, why not change his morality? Why not his very being? If you can twist the pronoun, why not the noun? If you revise his "I," why not his "AM"? Priestesses are merely the camel's nose under the tent. If it is admitted, the rest of the camel will follow, because it is a one-piece camel.

My previous point concerned the masculinity of God. The other half of the case against priestesses based on sexual symbolism is the femininity of the Church.

The Church is God's Bride. All the saints and mystics say the ultimate purpose of human life, the highest end for which we were made, is the Spiritual Marriage. This is not socially relative; it is eternal. And in it, the soul is spiritually impregnated by God, not vice versa. That is the ultimate reason why God must always be *he* to us, never *she*. Religion is essentially heterosexual and therefore fruitful.

The new birth—our salvation—comes from above, from without, from transcendence. We do not spiritually impregnate ourselves with salvation or divine life any more than we physically impregnate ourselves. Modernism, humanism, and naturalism amount to spiritual auto-eroticism, spiritual masturbation.

The Church can no more be fruitful without being impregnated by her Divine Husband than a woman can be impregnated with new life without a man. Feminists who resent this *fact,* resent this fact, and thus tend to resent facts as such, including their own nature as feminine.

The issue of priestesses is ultimately an issue of God. There have been three basic theological options, historically: the single transcendent Divine Husband (theism), many imminent gods and goddesses (paganism), or the pantheistic Divine Neuter or Hermaphrodite. Priestesses have always served the latter two gods, never the former. Deny God's transcendence, which is the condition for his revelation, and you get a lesbian Church, declaring independence from God as The Other, God as transcendent, God as masculine, believing herself to be already innately in possession of divine life, that is, denying Original Sin, or trying to impregnate herself horizontally by a kind of perverse auto-eroticism, narcissism, and self-idolatry. Lesbians, like gays, simply cannot make life, and the lesbian spirit of Womynchurch will never be able to make life without God the Father. The Christian saints and mystics have constantly used the scriptural and authoritative heterosexual metaphor of God as Husband to the Church and to the soul.

God made the Jews different and was extremely ornery and cantankerous about them remaining different, even to the extent of demanding the wholesale slaughter of pagan populations in the Promised Land to prevent them from corrupting his pure revelation to the Jews. Is this true? Is this divine revelation? Is this data? There it is, right in the very politically incorrect Bible. If God did not invent the Jews, then the Jews invented God. In that case, let's all be honest and cease to be Christians, or even theists, and become atheists, pagans, or pantheists, as many radical feminists have already done. Their spiritual gravity toward these three false religions is natural. And it is the agenda behind priestesses.

The obvious and ubiquitous objection to this view is that it is male chauvinism. To quote my colleague Mary Daly, "If God is male, then the male is God."[4] Besides the logical fallacy of the illicit conversion of an A proposition, I see five other mistakes in this argument—the first and most obvious of which is her claim that Judaeo-Christian tradition claims that God is male. It does not. God is masculine, not male. Women as much as men represent the image of God (cf. Gn 5.1–2). But at the heart of divine revelation is the simple fact that the First Person of the Trinity has chosen to reveal himself to us as Father. This is a category which transcends human biology (male and female), and of which human fatherhood is a shadow (cf. Eph 3.14).

Second, another essential part of the Christian data is the fact that the Eternal Word chose to incarnate and reveal himself as the Son of the

Father and Bridegroom of God's People. In order for a human to be a son or a bridegroom, he must be male. Jesus Christ is male because he is Son, not vice versa, as feminists assume. His choice does not constitute an insult to women, nor does it imply "an alleged natural superiority of man over woman," yet it "cannot be disassociated from the economy of salvation."[5] For it was part of the divine plan from the beginning for God to covenant himself to a people as a groom covenants himself to a bride. Christ is the Bridegroom, the Church is his Bride. This makes us all feminine in relation to God. Women need not become like men when they approach God, but men must become like women, spiritually. All souls are Christ's brides.

Third, Julie Loesch Wiley argues that if Jesus had been born a woman in the male-dominated world of the first century, his life and teaching of unselfish love for others would not have been as arresting and as instructively scandalous as it was. For women, in all times and places and cultures until modern feminism, have always been in general more altruistic, less power-greedy, less violence-prone, more self-emptying, and more naturally religious than men. (You still see more women than men in church.) In becoming a man, Jesus in a sense let women be and went after men to transform them—not into women, and certainly not into wimps, but into men like himself. He redefined manliness and power as the courage to suffer instead of the lust to dominate; giving instead of taking. Women were a little less in need of that lesson. Christianity seems closer to female chauvinism than to male.

The Incarnation was the *kenosis,* the "emptying." The Son of God came down to the lowest place, a crucified criminal in a Roman-occupied hick town—not an angel or an emperor, and not a woman. The Incarnation was not into privilege and power, but into suffering and service, and it was into a male. It is the modern feminists who are the real male chauvinists, lusting for reproductive freedom (sexual irresponsibility) like playboys and demanding empowerment, that is, envying and imitating not only males, but male fools, judging inner worth by outer performance, sacrificing being for doing, finding their identity in their worldly careers, not in their inner essence, in their physical and spiritual wombs and motherhoods. This is what Karl Stern called "the flight from woman." It is a strange and sad phenomenon. Genuinely hurt women often become radical feminists, hating their own femininity and hating ordinary women who love and enjoy their ordinary femininity. How often have you heard radical feminists praise midwestern housewives?

Fourth, women priests would demean and insult women, for it would be like asking them to be cross-dressers or to wear male sex organs. It would remove the distinctive dignity of women qua women as symbols of the Church, whom Christ, symbolized by the priest, marries. A symbol or sign is to be looked along, not looked at. What would priestesses mean, what would they symbolize? They would signify to all women that they are spiritual lesbians instead of brides.

Fifth, Christ's maleness is not chauvinistic because he had a mother (but no earthly father). Mary is the definitive refutation of the charge of chauvinism. No merely human being was ever nearly as great as this woman, according to the distinctive teachings of this "chauvinistic" Church. Mary is "our tainted nature's solitary boast."

"Mother of God" is hardly a title to sneer at! Mother of *anyone* is hardly a title to sneer at. A boy and girl were arguing about who would play captain in a game of pirates. The boy insisted on being captain; the girl won the argument by agreeing: "Okay, you can be the captain. But I'm the mother of the captain!"

The ground of Mary's greatness is the thing so simple and innocent that it is too simple and innocent for the feminists to see. The reason she is crowned Queen of Heaven, the reason for her great glory and power is her total submission to God—her sacrifice, her suffering, her service. Muslims see it, but so-called "Christian" feminists do not. It is *islam,* the total surrender, the *fiat,* and the peace, the *shalom,* that are the secret treasures hidden in this submission, the delicious fruit of this thorny plant. Modern feminist "Christianity" becomes radically different from Christianity (or Judaism or Islam) when it drifts into a radically different ideal of sanctity, of the *summum bonum,* the greatest good, meaning of life, and purpose of all faith. Feminists need most fundamentally what we all need most fundamentally: to go to the cross, unclench the fist, and bow the knee.

Reasons of the Common Good

My next four reasons against priestesses are reasons of the common good. Let's be practical for a moment. In terms of the concrete life of the Church, what would a Church with priest-esses look like?

To answer this question, we must back up and ask, "What is the relation between a priest and the Church?" The answer to that question is clearly, "The priest is for the Church, not the Church for the priest." The priesthood is not for personal fulfillment and certainly not for em-powerment. So the justification for changing the priesthood to include "priestesshood" must be the improvement of the laity, not the improve-ment of the priesthood.

Improvement in what direction? It has to be in the direction the Church is *for.* What is its end? Why did God make it? Not to be politi-cally correct (or politically incorrect), not to fulfill and happify and empower individuals (and not to stultify or unhappify or disempower indi-viduals either), but to save and to sanctify souls. That is the standard by which everything in the Church must be judged, from bingo to Opera-tion Rescue, from ecumenical councils to collection plates.

Now, what effect would the ordination of women have on salvation and sanctity? For one thing, it would undermine many Catholics' confidence in the Church's authority by contradicting the explicit teaching and universal practice of nineteen hundred years of history. Even if "no priestesses" is not *ex cathedra,* to begin to ordain women would surely create in many minds this question: "If the Church was wrong for almost two thousand years about this, why might not she be wrong about the rest of her ordinary teaching too?" It might well even foster doubt of Christ's wisdom and infallibility; for the Church's stand against priestesses, like her stand against divorce, is not based on her own idea or her own authority, but on her fidelity to Christ's. If Jesus goofed in being so chauvinistic as not to ordain apostlesses, why might he not also have been wrong and prejudiced and less enlightened than we are about other things, such as adultery and marriage, or even how to get to heaven?

Second, many of the faithful, in doubting the validity of women's ordination, would doubt the validity of all the sacraments received from priestesses. Are my sins forgiven? Perhaps not, if a priestess gave me absolution, or a priest ordained by a priestess-bishop. Is this really Christ I receive in the Eucharist, consecrated by a priestess, or am I blasphemously and idolatrously adoring a matzo?

Third, de facto schism would result—or at least enormous parish hopping, and the end of the geographical parish and the substitution of the ideological parish.

Fourth, it would tear apart the Church worldwide, for nearly all cultures, except the American, Canadian, and Western European cultures, are totally opposed to women's ordination. This is clear repeatedly at international conferences and synods of bishops. Third World Catholics would be deeply scandalized and probably form breakaway churches. The Lefevrite tragedy would be compounded a thousand times. The Church could be irredeemably fractured from its own tradition and therefore against itself. The Church could be as badly split as in 1054 or 1517.

So, for practical and prudential reasons, priestesses would be an ecclesiastical disaster.

And for principled reasons of Church order too. For feminists fail to understand what a priest is, not only sacramentally and symbolically, as we have already seen, but ecclesially and socially too. There is only one reason to be a priest: because one is called by God. Now how does one know the will of God? The only public, objective, and certain way to know the will of

God is by divine revelation. And God has revealed through the Church what he wants his priesthood to be. Anyone who does not believe that the Church's teachings are God's revelation is simply not a Catholic.

God has not let important things like the sacraments of his Church depend on our feelings or opinions. We can talk back to our Mother the Church, but she always has the last word because she is God's mouth. The Church tells us that the priesthood is not a right, and not a privilege. No one can claim the right to be a priest. She also tells us that priesthood is for the service of others, not for personal advantage, not even personal holiness. Being a priest does not make one better or holier necessarily. When it does, that is only a side effect of its main business, which is to make the laity better and holier.

Advocates of priestesses usually argue that to deny a woman this function is to insult her personal worth. This is the error of functionalism, the confusion of personal worth with function—like the arguments that justify early abortions or euthanasia by pointing out that the brain is not functioning rationally. This mistake, by the way, is more typical of males than females, for men have always tended to identify themselves and their worth with their jobs, or their achievements, while women have always (up until now) tended the traditional wisdom that being is deeper than doing.

Over ninety-nine per cent of all men also do not function as priests, and many of them cannot, by reason of age or physical or mental condition. Are they, therefore, less worthy and valuable human beings? If not, then neither are women, for the same reason.

Neither can a woman be a biological father. Is that also a slap in the face at her dignity? Has nature already insulted women in the same way the Church insults them? The more radical feminists will gladly answer yes, thus revealing their own fragile (and male) sense of self-worth. The others are hard-pressed to justify blaming the Church but not blaming nature. Neither nature nor the Church is simple-mindedly egalitarian.

The most egregious error of all is a demand to be priestesses for "empowerment." I can think of no term that more perfectly proves the speaker's utter incomprehension of what she says than that. It is like wanting to manage the Boston Red Sox because of a thirst for "success."

Priests are not power brokers or managers. They are sewers. Like Christ, they drain off the world's sins. They are spiritual garbage men. Like Christ, they clean up our spiritual garbage. They wash feet—dirty, smelly souls—ours. The Pope, priest of priests, is *servus servoram Dei,* servant of the servants of God. This is not a clever P. R. slogan, this is his real job description. Even if all my other reasons against priestesses were invalid, their advocates' total misunderstanding of a priest's essential job description would invalidate priestesses.

Reasons of Discernment

This bring me to my fourth, and last, and shortest kind of argument against priestesses: reasons of discernment. Can we discern what spirit is at work here?

I don't think we need to be very advanced in the Christian art of discernment to answer that question. All we need to do is listen, and if we listen with a heart open to God rather than to human ideology, we will easily hear the anger, the rage, the self-righteousness. If you don't know what I'm talking about, read Donna Steichen's *Ungodly Rage: The Hidden Face of Catholic Feminism.*

Who are the advocates of women's ordination? The most prominent and vocal are always dissenters against other official Church teachings as well. The issue of women's ordination is not an isolated issue; it is one thread of a seamless garment. Pull its thread and you pull the whole robe. (By the way, "dissenter" is just a modern euphemism for "heretic": one who says no, one who picks and chooses for himself, one who refuses to eat all the food Mommy tells us to eat.) Most shockingly, most feminists who advocate priestesses are usually also strong advocates of abortion. That fact seems to me immediately and totally to destroy all their credentials to a hearing. For we know what god the priestesses of abortion serve, and his name is not Jesus. His name is Moloch. Moloch also says, "Suffer the little children to come unto me," but where Jesus places his hand, Moloch places his teeth.

In addition to approving of abortion, the leaders of the push for priestesses also want the Church to approve contraception, fornication, sodomy, same-sex marriage, and divorce. A more complete demonic attack on the family could not possibly be orchestrated, even in hell. Some of the leaders in the movement, such as in Womynchurch, clearly admit that they are worshipping another god, Mother Earth, and practicing another religion, paganism—Christ's old enemy risen from the dead. Anyone who freely opens the Church's doors to these barbarians is clearly a traitor. Anyone who cannot see through these spies' tissue-thin cover of "Catholicism" is a fool.

The origin of modern feminism is not inside Christianity, but outside it in deeply anti-religious and anti-Christian ideologies like Marxism and deconstructionism. Mary Daly summarized her self-image candidly when she called herself (in *Pure Lust)* "the Antichrist," and summarized her life's work as "castrating God the Father." Next to her, Nietzsche was a wimp.

There is an obvious connection between the *root* of modern feminism, which is *not* prayer, personal holiness, or submission to God's will, and the *fruit,* which is *not* love or joy or peace. Look at their faces; you can see the hate, the hardness, the hurt. Not all advocates of priestesses have that look, but the leaders of the movement do.

In the *Spiritual Exercises,* St. Ignatius says that we must discern between the spirit of consolation (which is from God) and the spirit of desolation (which is from Satan). The latter produces these fruits: hate, anxiety, fear, resentment, anger, anguish, bitterness, rage, pain, and lack of peace. By their own admission, these are precisely the feelings of those in the forefront of the demand for women's ordination!

This is not a passing mood but a settled state of deep alienation. And these are not the feelings of a few individuals but of the movement itself, its very ideology. We can easily discern in feminists a past history of having been badly hurt—often sexually abused—which then became a state of deep hatred. Often it is a paradoxical mixture of great self-hatred and great self-righteousness. At the very least it includes great doses of self-pity, which certainly does not come from God.

Spiritual warfare is our condition at all times, according to Scripture and the saints, but especially today in this time of crisis and decadence in both Church and society. The issue of priestesses ultimately is a battle in this great war, a battle between the priests of the Lord and the priests of Baal, like Elijah's battle on Mount Carmel. It is a time for choosing—not just between theologies but between Gods; a time for repeating Joshua's challenge to Israel (remember "Joshua" means Jesus, and the Church is the new Israel): "Now therefore fear the LORD, and serve him in sincerity and faithfulness; put away the gods which your fathers served beyond the River, and in Egypt, and serve the LORD. And if you be unwilling to serve the LORD, choose this day whom you will serve, whether the gods your fathers served in the region beyond the River, or the gods of the Amorites in whose land you dwell; but as for me and my house, we will serve the LORD" (Jos 24.14–15).[6]

Endnotes to Part I

[1]Thomas Aquinas, *Summa Theologica,* I.1.10.

[2]C. S. Lewis, "Priestesses in the Church?" *God in the Dock* (Grand Rapids: Eerdmans, 1970), 236–238.

[3]C. S. Lewis, *Miracles* (New York: Macmillan, 1947; reprint, 1955), 113–114 (page citations are to reprint edition).

[4]Mary Daly, *Beyond God the Father* (Boston, 1974), 19.

[5]*Inter Insigniores,* Sacred Congregation, 15 October 1976, n. 28.

[6]RSVCE.

II

The Mystery of Femininity

Why It Excludes the Priesthood

by Alice von Hildebrand

The War against Women

If you want to kill a person, aim at his heart. If you want to destroy marriage, the family, the Church and society at large, wage war on femininity. This is precisely the aim of contemporary feminism; for this reason, Cardinal Ratzinger calls it one of the greatest dangers menacing the Church today. The Devil himself is hoisting the black flag and directing the operations. His plan of attack can only be detected and counteracted by faith, prayer, and sacrifice—in a word, by supernatural means.

Many of us have been led to believe that the feminist movement is a legitimate response to crying injustices perpetrated against women, but Donna Steichen's book *Ungodly Rage*[1] undermines this thesis. Feminism is in fact a radical attack on femininity. Chesterton wrote, "The Feminist . . . [is] one who dislikes the chief feminine characteristics."[2] For this reason, these women advocate a "unisex" attitude, which not only eliminates charm, poetry, and mystery from human life, but also runs counter to biblical teaching: "male and female he created them." Feminism defies the divine plan, accusing the Creator of "having goofed," and steers in the direction of perfect identity between male and female. In order to accomplish this aim, women must achieve control over their biological reproductivity, by means of artificial birth control, and when this fails, by abortion.

Women's clothes today ape male attire. Women copy male behavior—they now drink like men, curse like men, and imitate slavishly all the least attractive characteristics of the stronger sex. This in turn encourages men to abandon the chivalrous tradition of the past, and replace it with a chumminess which opens the door to vulgarity. Chesterton expressed this truth in his own inimitable fashion: "I remember an artistic and eager lady asking me . . . whether I believed in comradeship between the sexes, and why not." Chesterton responded, "Because if I were to treat you for two minutes like a comrade you would turn me out of the house."[3]

A man will respond to a woman either with respect or with contempt, with reverence or with lust. Women have the power to draw out of men what is best in them and kindle purity in their souls, or awaken what is worst in them and fuel in them the ever-rampant furnace of lust. A man who sees a woman whose body language has a note of holy modesty (which is not to be confused with prudishness) will inevitably feel awe in front of her, and will understand that her very presence calls him to adopt a reverent attitude. A woman whose body language expresses shamelessness and vulgarity actually invites the men who see her to unchaste thoughts and coarse behavior. All women should meditate on St. Paul's Epistle to Timothy, in which he admonishes women to "adorn themselves modestly" (1 Tm 2.9). He is referring to a secret confided to women, and this secret can only be guarded by holy pudor. Alas, this sense for the mystery of femininity is so lost today that pious and good young girls seem totally unaware that their way of dressing is often incompatible with their calling.

Second-Class Citizens

There is little doubt that the argument used by feminists is that women have been and are unfairly treated by men. Chesterton acknowledges that "women have been wronged and even tortured,"[4] but the difference between this great thinker and feminists is that "[he] want[s] to destroy the tyranny. They want to destroy the womanhood."[5]

Unfortunately some men view women purely as objects of physical satisfaction; this attitude is not only deplorable but is to be severely condemned and censured. Alas, this "mistreatment" is not limited to the physical sphere.

Some males suffer from the "macho superiority complex"; they assume that their very sex places them higher than "mere females," and so they enjoy stressing the alleged inferiority of the weaker sex. This baneful attitude is found even among intellectuals. Imagine the arrogance (and stupidity) of raising the question "Do women have a soul?"[6] It is tempting for women to raise the question of whether such a theologian has a brain. Other thinkers (and very great ones) have claimed that women should be ashamed of their sex.[7] Aristotle calls the female a "misbegotten male"[8];and St. Thomas Aquinas endorses this unfortunate thesis.[9]

But misbegotten and misshapen males are nonetheless indispensable in order to beget well-shaped ones. Without the misbegotten ones, the perfect exemplars would disappear surprisingly fast. This simply shows that great minds are not always at their best and we must forgive them. Indeed, humor has a role to play in the reading of some theological treatises.

Albeit totally unwarranted, metaphysical haughtiness is clearly a consequence of original sin which negatively affects women; for, sadly enough, telling a young girl repeatedly that she is unintelligent, limited, and incapable creates unfavorable soil for the blossoming of her talents.

The Church herself (as opposed to Churchmen) has always upheld the greatness and dignity of woman; as a matter of fact, she grants the "weaker sex" a cardinal role in the Economy of Redemption. In spite of this undeniable fact, feminists insist that the Catholic Church is responsible for the newly-discovered sin of "sexism" which has victimized Catholic women.

Let us review some of the arguments used by feminists to prove this point. They base their initial position on Genesis. Since Eve was created after Adam, she was meant to be what Simone de Beauvoir calls "the second sex." According to feminists, then, Genesis teaches that whereas Adam was the full human being, Eve was at best an afterthought. She was meant to be his helper, and therefore was, from the very beginning, in a position of inferiority. The result is that naive Catholic women have willingly submitted to and suffered from oppression by an exclusively male (read "sexist") hierarchy these past two thousand years.

This interpretation of Genesis is easily challenged. For Genesis tells us that God first created inanimate matter, then plants, then lower animals, then higher animals, then man, and finally woman. As there is a clear ascending line in creation, I personally cannot conceive why to be created last is a sign of metaphysical inferiority. Furthermore, Eve's body was taken from Adam's rib; feminists consider this demeaning. I, on the contrary, interpret this to manifest a woman's dignity. For to have one's body formed from the body of a person made in God's image and likeness grants one a very special nobility. No reasonable person would rather have his body fashioned from the dust of the earth—a very modest origin indeed.

We are told that God created Eve because "it was not good for man to be alone." To be created for the sake of love and companionship certainly is not an indication of imperfection; on the contrary, it clearly points to the fact that love is to play a crucial role in a woman's life. It is said further that "the man will leave his father and mother and join his wife" (Gn 2.24). Surprisingly enough, it is not written: "The woman will leave her father and mother . . . "

Saint Augustine claims that the serpent addressed himself to the woman because, being the weaker sex, she was easier to seduce. May I venture to challenge the view of a doctor of the Church, and suggest that, on the contrary, the serpent, being extremely astute, knew full well that once he had conquered Eve, Adam would follow suit. This is exactly what happened: the Bible does not tell us that he—the head of mankind—put up any kind of courageous resistance.

Original Sin had catastrophic consequences for both culprits: Adam and Eve both lost the gift of supernatural life and their preternatural gifts, and they both became subject to suffering and death. Yet in addition to these punishments, Adam was cursed to earn his bread by the sweat of his brow (a penalty which Eve often shares with him); while Eve was condemned to carry her offspring in pain and give birth in anguish (a burden which Adam does not share at all). Moreover Eve was made subject to her husband.

The role that men play in begetting children is not a difficult one; there is actually a shocking discrepancy between the role of the male and the role of the female in procreation. From a purely naturalistic point of view, this hardly seems fair. But when we abandon a naturalistic perspective, and read the Holy Scriptures with eyes open to the supernatural, we understand the profound meaning of the role which women have been assigned in the Economy of Redemption. All women are called upon to participate with Mary in her role as co-redemptrix, and to shed light on both the redeeming value of suffering and the deep link existing between love and suffering in human life.

Genesis tells us explicitly that it is a woman—not a man—who will crush the serpent's head. The sublime dialogue of the Annunciation takes place between the Angel Gabriel and the Virgin Mary. Saint Joseph, to whom she is engaged, is not even apprised of the amazing event which has taken place. It is only later, when he notices that Mary is with child, that an Angel of the Lord informs him of what has taken place in his holy fiancée. Saint Joseph is and remains totally in the background.

And yet Joseph, he who is tainted with Original Sin, is head of the Holy Family. This fact teaches us that to command does not point in any way to superiority and to obey does not point to inferiority: for Christ—the Second Person of the Holy Trinity—was subject to his parents. What a sublime subject of meditation for women.

At Calvary, women are once again in the foreground of this unfathomable drama. Thomas, who had ventured to say at the time of the resurrection of Lazarus, "Let us go and die with him," fled when Christ was arrested, together with Peter who had solemnly declared a few hours earlier that he would give his life for Christ. As a matter of fact, all of the Apostles fled. Saint John later changed his mind and was at the foot of the Cross with Mary, the Mother of the Crucified, and the Holy Women who had followed Christ all the way to Golgotha because their love overcame fear. It is true that a man, Simon of Cyrene, helped Christ carry his cross, yet St. Luke tells us explicitly that Simon did not volunteer to do so, but was forced to help our Savior. He might even have grumbled at the task, but nevertheless he did do it.

On Easter Sunday, Christ first appeared to Mary Magdalene. Yes, women were the first to receive the overwhelming news of the Resurrection, without which our faith would be in vain (cf. 1 Cor 15.14). But when the Holy Women informed the Apostles of this tremendous event, the latter discounted it as "women's talk." They refused to believe that Christ had risen, even though he had clearly predicted both his passion and his resurrection. Once again, the glorious role of women is highlighted in the Gospels.

In the Apocalypse, a "duel" takes place between the woman "clothed with the sun, with the moon under her feet, and on her head a crown of twelve stars" (12.1), and the dragon who tries to devour the fruit of her womb. This symbolizes the triumph of Mary—the new Eve—over Satan. He conquered Eve; but he will be defeated by Mary, the blessed one among women.

A supernatural reading of the Holy Scriptures gives women a reason to rejoice: indeed we have been assigned a privileged role in the story of redemption. For we are called upon to emulate Mary who alone deserves to be called Co-Redemptrix.

The Mystery of Femininity

Women are definitely more mysterious than men, not only because their affective life is more complex and more refined, but especially because there is something in women that calls for veiling. It is not by accident that women traditionally wore a veil, and that, up to Vatican II, they wore veils in Catholic churches. This custom was deeply symbolic, and alas this symbolism is now lost. Under the influence of feminism, many Catholics were led to believe that veiling indicated some sort of inferiority, and for this reason it was abolished.

This interpretation rests on a misunderstanding. Far from indicating inferiority, the veil points to sacredness. While we do cover what is ugly or decaying, we also veil what is sacred, mysterious, and sublime. When Moses came down from Mount Sinai, he covered his face to hide the glow that was apparent because God had deigned to speak with him: Moses' body reflected the depth and mystery of his experience.

Every woman carries within herself a secret most sacred, mysterious, and sublime. This secret is life. Eve means "the mother of the living." In the mystery of the female body, human life finds its beginning: not in the male semen but in the fecundated egg, hidden in the cavern of the female body. There God creates a new soul which is exclusively his work, and in which neither father nor mother has a part. This creation takes place when the male seed fecundates the female egg. Thus at that very moment a closeness exists between divine action and the female body which marks the latter as sacred ground. This is why the way that a woman dresses, the way she sits, walks, laughs, should always be marked by a note of holy reserve. A woman conscious of her unmerited privilege will necessarily adopt a bodily posture—what is today called body language—which adequately reflects this calling.

As Christ has said, "I am the way, the truth, and the life," once again we see how privileged women are according to the divine plan. The Christian woman knows that she is called upon to give not only physical life, but that she is especially called to help the fruit of her womb find the true life which is Christ himself. As Paul Evdokimov puts it: she is called upon to help (with God's grace) engender souls to eternal life.[10]

Woman fulfills her amazing vocation not through exterior accomplishments, but through prayer, sacrifice, and love.

Women are notoriously more pious than men; we need only visit churches in Latin countries to see that women outnumber men. Around

1900 the French Academy offered an award to the person who best answered the question, "Why are there more men than women in jails?" The award was given to the person who wrote: "Because there are more women than men in churches." Today it is a well known fact that faith in communist Russia was safeguarded by women.[11]

Women tend to be more pious than men because they are by nature more receptive, and receptivity is the key to holiness; one becomes a saint not by "efficiency," but by total acceptance of God's grace, and a total "yes" to his plans for us. Saint Augustine expressed this truth in the famous words: "Da quod jubes; et jube quod vis (Give what you command; and command what you will)."[12] All one has to do is to say "yes." This is strikingly illustrated in the Old and New Testaments. The little Samuel in the temple answered to God's call with the words: "Speak, O Lord, thy servant listens" (listening is receptive). And the Holy Virgin's response to the Annunciation was: "I am the handmaid of the Lord; be it *done* to me according to thy word."

The male temptation of activism, of uncontemplative creativity, is, by the way, a temptation to which women were not exposed until feminism convinced some of them that "being" means "doing." In fact, this is a heresy that was condemned by Leo XIII under the title Americanism.

Moreover, women, being physically weaker than men, are more conscious of their creature-liness, and creatures are metaphysically so dependent that they are constantly in need of help. How easily the words "Help me, O Lord, lest I perish" come to a woman's lips. A woman who gives birth prays, because in this supreme moment she experiences through a striking para-dox both the amazing privilege granted to her and the humbling precariousness of her situa-tion. In giving birth, she faces death, both for herself and for the beloved fruit of her womb.

When piety dies out in women, society is threatened in its very fabric; for a woman's re-lationship to the sacred keeps the Church and society on an even keel, and when this link is severed, both are threatened by total moral chaos. Once again the menace of feminism lurks in the background. The ravages which it is cre-ating in our society can hardly be gauged. Poisoned by a wrong philosophy, some women now trample upon the mystery of their femininity and willingly collaborate with men in committing one of the most brutal of all crimes: the murder of the defenseless unborn. Terrible as the crime of the abortionist is, the crime of the aborter is truly unfathomable: for the woman not only assists in a murder, she betrays her very vocation to give life, becoming instead an apostle of death.

This must be why the great Danish philosopher Kierkegaard wrote that women are either better or worse than men: "If one would indicate the weakest, the most feeble thing, one says 'a woman'; if one would give a notion of a spiritual quality raised above all sensuousness, one says 'a woman'; . . . if one would indicate innocence in all its lofty greatness, one says 'a woman'; if one would point to the depressing feeling of guilt, one says 'a woman.'"[13]

In *The Scarlet Letter* by Hawthorne, the heroine Hester Prynne, mother of an illegitimate child, is condemned to carry the letter "A" on her breast to make everyone aware of her shame, inviting all to show contempt for her degradation. The history of mankind testifies to the fact that women were usually much more severely treated than men for a sin which by its very nature calls for two partners. In several societies men were, and in some still are, easily excused for their unchaste behavior because, as one says, "they must sow their wild oats." Women, on the other hand, have often been treated with inhuman severity. Obviously fornication or adultery is of equal *moral* gravity whether it is committed by a man or by a woman. But the social censures to which we have alluded indicate that deep down societies acknowledge the fact that women—having received a sacred calling—are particularly accountable for any deviation from this noble vocation; unchaste behavior on the part of a woman amounts to a betrayal of a trust given to her by God. For this reason impure women were and are looked down upon as contemptible, despicable, and shameful, and often in the most ruthless and uncharitable ways. (Today the tendency is to show greater compassion toward such women, but unfortunately this goes hand in hand with a denial that sins of the flesh are grave offenses against God.)

No doubt, a woman is more deeply affected by unchaste behavior than is a man. The enamel of her soul is more severely scratched by this type of sin than his, for a man can better separate his mind from his heart, and usually does not give himself in the same fashion. This male capacity to divorce mind and emotions is both an advantage and a disadvantage. It is expedient when an objective judgment is called for. But it also points to a dichotomy in a man's soul that needs to be corrected and can best be healed by a deep religious life.

* * *

Women play such a crucial role in both society and the Church that it is not surprising that the Devil is now waging a fierce war on femininity, and particularly on the greatness of motherhood. It is he who has inspired the philosophy of feminism which calls marriage "obscene,"[14] the fetus "a parasite,"[15] and interprets giving birth as a purely biological event which is more efficiently performed by rats and rabbits.[16] This philosophy effectively singles out maternity as the one great obstacle preventing women from developing their talents and reaching what the French mother of feminism calls "transcendence."

It is true that men have been the great creators in music, architecture, painting, philosophy, theology, the sciences, technology, etc. But two remarks are called for. First, human persons are to be gauged not according to what they produce (as de Beauvoir claims), but according to who they *are.* In eternity we shall not be judged according to whether or not we have invented great things or victoriously led armies to conquer the earth. We shall be judged according to the measure of our love for God and for our neighbors. Moreover, St. Peter tells us that the world will perish by a fire that will destroy all things (cf. 2 Pt 3.10). All human creations, beautiful as they are, will turn to ashes at the end of the world. Not a single human accomplishment will survive this total destruction, except every child born of a woman, because God has given each an immortal soul and the promise of bodily resurrection. The woman is once again placed on a metaphysical pedestal: for what she "produces" will escape destruction. And yet Simone de Beauvoir dares claim that she "produces nothing."[17]

*   *   *

We live in a world that is becoming less and less human, more and more heartless: a world dominated by technology, by machines, which are essentially "masculine." This is particularly true of hospitals where it is now most difficult to meet humans. Everything is ruled by machines, which cannot smile or utter a word of comfort to the sick who are desperately in need of kindness, understanding, patience, and mercy in order to carry the burden of suffering allotted to them. Each human person is made of body and soul, and the body cannot recover from disease when the soul is ignored. Mother Teresa has often said that spiritual destitution is more detrimental to man than acute physical need. Technology is certainly not to be abandoned, but unless it is "corrected" by the feminine element of empathy, it will have disastrous effects.

Empathy is the very special charism given to women and particularly women religious who, in the past, have been the joy and comfort of innumerable suffering people. Unfortunately today's climate not only discourages religious vocations, but actually encourages many nuns to abandon their vocations and turn to "more productive" occupations. The feminine element has been choked by feminism which has proclaimed that only masculine occupations lead to "self fulfillment." Unless we reverse what Karl Stern calls "flight from woman," our amazing technological advances will be our spiritual downfall. We desperately need both the masculine and the feminine principles. They complement each other. They belong together.

These remarks were meant to illumine the fact that the mystery of purity, of sex, of birth, is particularly confided to women. It is worth noting that in both the breviary and the missal when the feast of a male saint is celebrated he is listed as either pope, bishop, confessor, non-confessor, doctor of the Church, or martyr. When a female saint is honored, she is listed as virgin or non-virgin. Priests do take a vow of celibacy, but this is not mentioned when their feast is celebrated by the Church, indicating once again that the mystery of the sexual sphere is particularly confided to women.

The Priesthood

It is time to turn to the core of my topic: why women are excluded from the priesthood— a burning question for many Catholics, and a stumbling block for feminists who accuse the Church of a dreadful sin unknown until recently: sexism.

To place the question in its proper perspective, we should recall that through Original Sin we lost the unmerited gift of supernatural life; moreover, our intelligence was darkened, our will weakened, our heart hardened. Through the loving condescension of the God-man who assumed our human nature, not only has supernatural life been restored to us, but we have been offered a lesson in humility. The sin of our first parents was primarily a sin of pride; the redeeming action of the God-man was the most amazing gesture of humility. This is the divine cure offered to sinful man, but this virtue, learned and practiced through the acceptance of humiliations, is so distasteful to his fallen nature that to him it is worse than death. There is nothing he loathes more than to be humiliated; he dreads it even more than suffering. Indeed, very many people would prefer physical torture to being publicly humiliated. Our fallen nature is allergic to the cure our Savior has brought us.

It is typical of pride to revolt, to dissent, to refuse to bend its neck, to disobey a legitimate authority. The Old Testament records the story of a people in constant revolt because they resented the burdens that their divine election put upon their shoulders. One would expect that since Christians have a New Covenant which is a covenant of love, this rebellious tendency would be tamed. But alas, it is not the case. Christians rebel against the sweet burden of the supernatural. We are like the Gerasenes who begged Christ to leave their territory after they witnessed the miraculous healing of a man with an unclean spirit. One would expect these people to thank the Savior and beg him to remain with them. Far from it: they wanted him to depart; the supernatural had come uncomfortably close. How right Kierkegaard was when he wrote that we are all more or less afraid of the truth.[18] One of the saddest words in St. Paul's epistles is the one he addresses to the Galatians: "Have I then become your enemy by telling you the truth?" (4.16). Christ would not have been crucified if he had not brought sinful humanity the Truth that he himself was.

It is interesting to note that women who, thanks to God's grace, view the Church with the eyes of faith, would never dream of raising the question "Why can't we be ordained?" It is only when the supernatural has been brushed aside and obnubilated that this type of query is likely to spring up. As soon as one adopts a purely naturalistic point of view, it seems legitimate to ask: Why should women be excluded from holy functions? All human beings are equal in dignity. Why should men be placed above them? Why should a purely biological peculiarity prevent women from consecrating bread and wine and hearing confessions? Is not this prohibition indicative that the Church (ruled by men from the very beginning) is keeping women in an inferior position which is radically opposed to authentic Christian teaching? Does not St. Paul write that from now on "there is neither male nor female; for you are all one in Christ Jesus" (Gal 3.28)? That Christ did not ordain women is to be explained sociologically: he was bound by the customs of his time.

All of this sounds very convincing to an ear untuned to the supernatural, and alas, modern man has developed an allergy to its sublime message. Let us not forget that the supernatural is the warp and woof of Christianity; Christianity stands or falls with it. Given the "spirit of the time" which emphasizes man's maturity, man's craving for independence, it is particularly difficult to accept a teaching based on humility.

To be told that we should love our enemies, do good to those who persecute us (cf. Mt 5.44); that if anyone strikes us on the right cheek, we should turn to him the other also (cf. Mt 5.39); that we should give our tunic to the person who has already requested our cloak (cf. Mt 5.40; Lk 6.29); to be told that we should prefer to be defrauded than to have lawsuits (cf. 1 Cor 6.7): these are commands which sound discordant to the modern ear. Modern man is the enemy of the cross.

Blinded to the supernatural, feminists tell us that the Christian message should be re-interpreted in the light of modern scholarship which feeds on sociology and psychology. This information, they claim, is essential to understanding revelation. Their re-interpretation is cleverly done: before reaching its radical form, it progressively waters down the Christian message until finally (to quote Kierkegaard), "wine is changed into water." The supernatural is replaced by purely naturalistic categories which make it quite palatable to the spirit of the time. Through this process, St. Paul is praised as a genius,[19] and placed in the same category as an Einstein. Mother Teresa is praised as a great organizer and likened to a television mogul. The Holy Virgin is praised for her resiliency and vitality (she stood at the foot of the cross!). The Bishop of Chur (Switzerland)—handpicked by the Pope—is rejected by his congregation, one of the reasons being that he has no Ph.D., whereas the candidate that "the people" preferred (a liberal) has one!

How readily we forget that "God chooses weak things" (1 Cor 1.27): Moses stuttered and yet God chose him to go to Pharaoh (from a naturalistic point of view, it would have been a lot wiser to select an orator with Demosthenes' talents); St. Peter, a fisherman, denied Christ three times and nevertheless was chosen to be the first Pope; St. Paul, whose talents no one can deny, glorifies himself exclusively in his weakness (cf. 2 Cor 2.30). God's work is accomplished not by efficiency and talents, but by holiness, and there is no holiness without humility and an awareness that "without Christ we can do nothing." Indeed, we are useless laborers.

Christ said, "Blessed are those who are not scandalized in me" (Mt 11.6). Many were scandalized by his divine message because they refused to transcend purely naturalistic categories and open their minds and their hearts to the supernatural—a scandal to the Jews and foolishness to the Gentiles (cf. 1 Cor 1.23).

The United States bishops' document on women states repeatedly that "the latter will no longer tolerate to be treated as second-class citizens." Apparently many of the bishops were impressed by their plea "to be granted a place in the Church, where they feel alienated." But once again, the supernatural is out of court. Isaiah (often called the fifth Evangelist), prophesying about Christ, wrote, "He was despised and rejected, a man of sorrow, acquainted with grief, as one from whom men hide their faces. . . . He was oppressed and he was afflicted, yet he opened not his mouth" (Is 53.3, 7).

For the sake of argument, let us assume that women have in fact been unfairly treated in the Catholic Church. One possible response—the one of feminists—is bitterness and revolt leading progressively to a total rejection of the Christian message. The other is to meditate on the words of Isaiah and contemplate the life and death of the Savior of the world. He was ridiculed, slapped, spat upon, tortured, and crucified. It is understandable when someone rejects Christianity because its message is to take up one's cross and follow Christ. But it is un-understandable when people call themselves Christians while systematically rejecting the very core of Christianity: the imitation of Christ.

A Vocation of Loving Obedience

Inebriated with love of Christ, St. Thérèse of Lisieux understood in a unique fashion that to love Christ is to follow and imitate him. She admits in her autobiography that women are often scorned, and yet that very many of them love

God more than men do. "During our Lord's Passion," she writes, "women showed much more courage than the apostles; for they defied the soldiers' insults and dared wipe Jesus' adorable face. No doubt He allows that contempt should be their lot on this earth for this is what He has chosen for Himself. . . . In heaven, He will show that His thoughts are not those of men, and then the last will be the first."[20]

Women used to understand intuitively that it is a privilege to follow Christ to Calvary; today, thanks to the poison of feminism, many women are far more concerned about "fulfilling themselves" and receiving the recognition which is their due. For them, the supernatural is lost.

In giving many talks on feminism to feminists over the years, I have observed time and again that all the classical arguments against the ordination of women fall on rocky ground. To feminists these arguments not only lack plausibility, but actually serve to increase their opposition. If one tells them that it was God's will that males alone should be ordained, they accuse the Christian God of sexism. If one tells them that Christ did not choose his holy mother for the priesthood, they answer that he was imprisoned by the sociological categories prevalent at his time. If one reminds them of the fate of the Levite Korah who, with the support of Dathan and Abiram, protested against Moses' and Aaron's priestly authority, saying in effect: "How dare you place yourselves above us. All of us are priests, all of us are on the same level" (Nm 16.3), to which Moses responded, "Let God judge," after which the earth opened up and swallowed the rebels—nevertheless, feminists persist in their views.

If one uses a theological argument, such as the one propounded by Msgr. William Smith, that in every sacrament there are two essential factors, the matter and the form, and that the matter of the sacrament of holy ordination is the male sex, they view this argument as another proof that the Church is biased in her treatment of women.

Valuable as purely intellectual arguments are, we should realize that the problem is not an intellectual one; *it is a moral one.* No one will ever accept the validity of an argument he *chooses* not to accept; purity of heart is indispensable in order to be convinced by a solution which is unpalatable to one's pride and rebelliousness.

It was Mother Teresa of Calcutta who said that there was only one person on earth who could truly have said, "This is my body; this is my blood": the Holy Virgin; and she was not chosen to be an apostle and consequently a priest. Women—to whom is confided the mystery of life—are essentially called upon to be mothers (even when they have no physical fruit of their wombs); and many of them have had the privilege of being the mothers of priests. As Paul Evdokimov put it: mothers are called upon to help engender Christ in their children's souls, for it is often the mother who, by her suffering and love, leads her son to the priesthood. Let us recall the role played by Mamma Margarita in Don Bosco's vocation; let us remember the moving words that Cardinal Mindszenty dedicated to his saintly mother in his autobiography; how often have I heard a priest say that he owes his vocation to his grandmother or to his mother. The holiest priests I know have a very special devotion to the Holy Virgin, Mother of the Redeemer. Every priest needs a mother, even the Priest par excellence—Christ himself.

On Easter Sunday, Christ first appeared to Mary Magdalene—the person who probably loved him most after his mother; yet when she recognized him and cried out, "Rabboni!" he said to her, "Noli me tangere (Do not touch me)." Soon afterwards he appeared to the incredulous Thomas and told him to put his fingers in the wound of his side. She who loved him so ardently and followed him to Calvary was not permitted to touch his holy body; he who had fled from Golgotha and then doubted was invited to touch Christ's Holy Wounds. These facts should be meditated upon by those who challenge divine decisions.

One thing is certain: some women might believe themselves to be called to the priesthood, but this calling comes from their subjective wishes and not from the One who alone is to choose those whom he wants; it is always tempting for fallen man to assume that God's will matches his own will. These women are a far cry from the attitude of "the handmaid of the Lord"; they forget that the apostles did not choose to be apostles; they were chosen ("he called those he wanted," Mk 3.13). Mary did not choose to be God's mother; she was chosen, and said "yes."

To conclude, let me quote once again St. Thérèse of Lisieux who, in her autobiography, answers a question which in her day had yet to be asked. Carried by the intensity of her love for Christ, she exclaims that to be Christ's spouse, Carmelite, and mother of souls does not satisfy her longing. She also desires to be a warrior (for Christ), a priest, an apostle, a doctor, a martyr; she longs to accomplish for Jesus the most heroic deeds. She feels in her soul the courage of a crusader, of a pontifical Zouave; she would like to die on the battlefield for the Church.

Thérèse feels drawn to the priesthood, and tells us eloquently how lovingly she would carry Christ in her hands at the moment of consecration, and with what love she would give him to souls. But she adds that, while longing to be a priest, she admires the humility of St. Francis of Assisi in refusing the sublime dignity of the priesthood.

Her song of love reaches its climax in her desire to be a martyr and to shed her blood for her Beloved. Realizing the impossibility of uniting all these callings, she writes that she suffers tortures: for she cannot live up to her longing. But then by turning to the Epistle of St. Paul, she finds a sentence which gives her peace: "So faith, hope, love abide . . . but the greatest of these is love" (1 Cor 13.13). Thérèse then understands that *her vocation is love,* and that love combines all the various callings which she had longed to unite.[21]

Love was the calling of the Holy Virgin; it was also Thérèse's calling. Love is the calling addressed to all women, and the only appropriate response to this sublime vocation is to say with Mary, "I am the handmaid of the Lord; be it done to me according to thy word."

Endnotes to Part II

[1]Cf. Donna Steichen, *Ungodly Rage: The Hidden Face of Catholic Feminism* (San Francisco: Ignatius Press, 1991).

[2]G. K. Chesterton, *What's Wrong with the World* (New York: Dodd, Mead and Co., 1910), 223.

[3]Ibid., 176.

[4]Ibid., 160.

[5]Ibid., 225.

[6]Paul Evdokimov: "La Femme et le Salut du monde" (Casterman, 1958), 249.

[7]Cf. ibid., 167.

[8]Aristotle, *De Gener. Anim.,* II, 3.

[9]Cf. Thomas Aquinas, *Summa Theologica,* XLII.

[10]Cf. Paul Evdokimov: "La Femme et le Salut du monde" (Casterman, 1958), 264.

[11]Ibid.

[12]Augustine, *Confessions,* X.29.

[13]Søren Kierkegaard, *Either/Or: A Fragment of Life:* II, trans. D. F. Swenson and L. M. Swenson (Garden City, New York: Doubleday, 1959), 93–94.

[14]Simone de Beauvoir, *The Second Sex,* trans. and ed. H. M. Parshley (New York: Knopf, 1953), 444.

[15]Ibid., 495.

[16]Cf. ibid.

[17]Ibid., 456.

[18]*The Journals of Søren Kierkegaard,* trans. A. Dru (New York: Harper, 1959), 202.

[19]Cf. Søren Kierkegaard, *Of the Difference between a Genius and an Apostle,* trans. A. Dru (New York: Harper, 1962), 89.

[20]Thérèse of Lisieux, *Manuscrits Autobiographiques,* Manuscript A, Folio 66.

[21]Cf. Thérèse of Lisieux, *Manuscrits Autobiographiques,* Part II, Letter to Sister Marie of the Sacred Heart, Manuscript B, Folio 2ff.

DATE DUE

			Printed in USA